£39.98 free postage
Amazon

D1825938

PALEO

EASY VEGETABLES MEALS

50 NONSTARCHY VEGGIES DISHES

BALANCED WITH LEAN NATURAL PROTEINS

AND HEALTHY UNREFINED FATS

Marcel "The Caveman" Fortune

JUST4YOU EDITION

PALEO

EASY VEGETABLES MEALS

50 NONSTARCHY VEGGIES DISHES

BALANCED WITH LEAN NATURAL PROTEINS

AND HEALTHY UNREFINED FATS

Marcel "The Caveman" Fortune

JUST4YOU EDITION

TABLE OF CONTENTS

INTRODUCTION

THE ABUNDANCE AND THE VERSATILITY OF VEGETABLES OFFER INFINITE TASTES, TEXTURES, COLORS, AND FLAVORS. IMAGINE A MOUTHFUL OF FRESH LOCAL ORGANIC CARROTS AND ZUCCHINI WITH A HINT OF GARLIC AND A TOUCH OF GINGER. HOW ABOUT A BITE OF DELICATE BROCCOLI AND CAULIFLOWER FLORETS CARAMELIZED WITH ORANGE ZEST AND A HINT OF WALNUT OIL? PERHAPS A SIDE OF THYME-INFUSED SQUASH WITH TOMATO AND SLICED ALMONDS? YOU CAN ENJOY VEGGIES CRISP, FRESH, DELICIOUS, AND COOKED WITH EASE.

PREPARING VEGETABLES WITH A LIGHT TOUCH ENSURES THAT THEY DELIVER THEIR NUTRITIONAL BENEFITS TO YOU IN A TASTY WAY. JUST BECAUSE VEGETABLES CAN BE CONSIDERED NATURE'S PREVENTIVE MEDICINE DOESN'T MEAN THEY HAVE TO TASTE LIKE MEDICINE. VEGETABLES ARE A NET ALKALINE-YIELDING FOOD, WHICH MEANS THAT IF WE EAT THEM, OUR BODIES ARE FAR LESS LIKELY TO LOSE CALCIUM FROM OUR BONES, WHICH IN TURN HELPS US TO MAINTAIN STRONG SKELETONS. ON THE OTHER HAND, DIETS THAT ARE LOW IN VEGETABLES AND HIGH IN GRAINS, CHEESES, AND PROCESSED SALTY FOODS CREATE AN ACIDIC CONDITION IN THE BODY, WHICH MAY LEAD TO OSTEOPOROSIS, HIGH BLOOD PRESSURE, KIDNEY STONES, AND OTHER DISEASES OF ACID-ALKALI IMBALANCE.

EQUALLY IMPORTANT, VEGETABLES, WITH THEIR RICH SUPPLY OF VITAMINS, MINERALS, PHYTOCHEMICALS, ANTIOXIDANTS, AND FIBER, PLAY A HUGE PART IN HELPING US FIGHT HEART DISEASE AND CANCER. THESE PALEO NONSTARCHY CARBOHYDRATES ALSO HELP TO NORMALIZE BLOOD GLUCOSE AND INSULIN LEVELS, WHICH IN TURN PROMOTES WEIGHT LOSS AND DECREASES YOUR CHANCE OF DEVELOPING TYPE 2 DIABETES. IN ADDITION, EATING THESE IMPORTANT FOODS WILL KEEP YOU ENERGIZED ALL DAY LONG.

THE DISTINCTION BETWEEN LOW CARB AND LOW STARCH IS IMPORTANT. IT'S ONE OF THE SIGNIFICANT WAYS THE PALEO DIET DIFFERS FROM OTHER POPULAR DIETS. SOME LOW-CARB DIETS ADVISE THEIR FOLLOWERS TO MINIMIZE OR ELIMINATE CERTAIN, OR SOMETIMES ALL, CARBOHYDRATES, INCLUDING FRUITS AND VEGETABLES. THE PALEO DIET OFFERS LIMITLESS OPTIONS FOR EATING NONSTARCHY VEGGIES AND FRESH FRUIT, BALANCED WITH LEAN NATURAL PROTEINS AND HEALTHY UNREFINED FATS.

INCORPORATING VEGETABLES INTO YOUR DIET, COMBINED WITH ELIMINATING THE ANTINUTRIENTS FOUND IN GRAINS AND LEGUMES, ALLOWS YOUR BODY TO ABSORB ALL THE VITAMINS AND MINERALS THAT VEGGIES HAVE TO OFFER. YOU'LL FEEL SATISFIED WITHOUT FEELING STUFFED. THE DIVERSITY OF VEGETABLES THAT YOU MAY CHOOSE FROM IS ENORMOUS. TRY SOMETHING NEW. HAVE YOU EVER TASTED KOHLRABI OR BELGIAN ENDIVE? HOW ABOUT DAIKON RADISHES, BOK CHOY, OR BAMBOO SHOOTS? WE ENCOURAGE YOU TO EXPLORE ETHNIC MARKETS AND CHECK OUT THEIR PRODUCE SECTIONS. THE ONLY VEGETABLES THAT ARE TABOO ON THE PALEO

DIET ARE POTATOES, ALL BEANS, AND OTHER LEGUMES, FOR THE REASONS PREVIOUSLY MENTIONED. THERE ARE A FEW ADDITIONAL VEGETABLES THAT YOU MAY WANT TO AVOID.

ARE YOU NEW TO THE KITCHEN? UNSURE HOW TO USE THE OVEN AND RANGE? COOKING WITH VEGETABLES IS A GREAT WAY TO TEST THE WATERS. BECAUSE MOST VEGETABLES CAN SAFELY BE EATEN RAW, PREPARING THEM IS EASY. YOU DON'T HAVE TO WORRY ABOUT UNDERCOOKING THEM OR MAKING A BIG MISTAKE IN THE INGREDIENTS RATIOS, AS YOU DO WITH MEATS OR WHEN BAKING. VEGETABLE PREPARATION CAN BECOME SOMETHING THAT YOU AND EVEN YOUR KIDS CAN LEARN TO DO WITH EASE IN A VERY SHORT PERIOD. APPROACH IT PLAYFULLY AND PLAN ON HAVING FUN WITH THE CREATION AND CONSUMPTION OF EVERY NEW DISH.

OFTEN, WITH LITTLE MORE THAN GOOD OLIVE OIL AND A BIT OF SEA SALT, THE NATURALLY DELICIOUS flAVORS OF FRESH, SEASONAL PRODUCE SHINE.

LOCAL FARMER'S MARKETS ARE A VALUABLE RESOURCE FOR SOURCING EXCEPTIONAL VEGETABLES, AS YOU'LL ONLY BE ABLE TO PURCHASE WHAT'S CURRENTLY IN SEASON. SOON YOU'LL LEARN WHAT TIME OF YEAR TO EXPECT CERTAIN VEGETABLES AND HOW TO PLAN YOUR MENU ACCORDINGLY.

1. JULIENNED VEGGIE STIR-FRY

SIMPLY CUT YOUR VEGGIES INTO MATCHSTICKS USING A SHARP KNIFE. AN IMPORTANT PART OF THIS RECIPE, AND OF ALMOST ANY STIR-FRY, IS TO ALLOW THE VEGETABLES TO BROWN. ONCE THEY ARE ADDED TO THE PAN, LET A MINUTE OR SO PASS WITHOUT STIRRING.

SERVES 4

INGREDIENTS

2 TABLESPOONS EXTRA VIRGIN OLIVE OIL

1 TEASPOON GRATED FRESH GINGER

2 SCALLIONS, FINELY CHOPPED

1 TABLESPOON ORANGE ZEST

2 GARLIC CLOVES, MINCED

2 LARGE CARROTS, PEELED AND JULIENNED

1 RED BELL PEPPER, JULIENNED

2 MEDIUM YELLOW SQUASH, JULIENNED

2 MEDIUM ZUCCHINI, JULIENNED

DIRECTION

1. Heat oil in a cast iron skillet over medium flame and sauté ginger and scallions while stirring for two minutes.
2. Add orange zest and garlic and mix lightly for about one minute.
3. Toss in carrots and peppers.
4. Stir so that all veggies come in contact with the pan at some point and continue browning.
5. Leave veggies to cook for one additional minute without stirring.
6. Place the squash and zucchini in the pan and mix evenly for one minute. Cover and cook over medium heat for ten minutes; stir once.
7. Veggies are done when tender.
8. Remove from flame and let cool for two minutes.

2. SPAGHETTI SQUASH ITALIANO

SPAGHETTI SQUASH IS VERY HANDY AS A VEGETABLE SIDE DISH OR AS A BASE FOR PALEO SAUCE OR PROTEIN. HERE'S A SIMPLE RECIPE THAT IS TASTY ENOUGH TO BE ENJOYED ALONE BUT UNCOMPLICATED ENOUGH TO BE ADDED TO A MORE ADVENTUROUS MEAL.

SERVES 4

INGREDIENTS

1 MEDIUM SPAGHETTI SQUASH

1 TABLESPOON CHOPPED FRESH BASIL

1 TABLESPOON DRIED OREGANO

2 TABLESPOONS CHOPPED FRESH CILANTRO

1 TABLESPOON EXTRA VIRGIN OLIVE OIL

1 TABLESPOON FLAXSEED OIL

DIRECTION

1. Preheat oven to 425 degrees.
2. Halve spaghetti squash lengthwise.
3. Using a fork, remove seeds and discard.
4. Fill a large glass or ceramic baking dish with 1 inch of water.
5. Place both squash halves, cut side down, into pan.
6. Bake for forty minutes.
7. Squash is done when skin is easily pierced with a fork.
8. Remove squash from pan and set aside until cool enough to handle, for five to ten minutes.
9. Using a fork, scrape out the strands of squash, which will now resemble spaghetti, onto a large, flat serving dish.
10. In a small jar, combine basil, oregano, and cilantro with the two oils and shake well.
11. Pour over squash strands and mix well.

3. ROASTED BABY SQUASH AND CARROTS

BABY VEGETABLES ARE FULLY RIPE, MINIATURE VEGETABLES, CULTIVATED TO PERFECTION. THEY OFTEN HAVE A SWEETER TASTE THAN THEIR LARGER COUNTERPARTS.

SERVES 4

INGREDIENTS

2 TABLESPOONS EXTRA VIRGIN OLIVE OIL

1 OR 2 GARLIC CLOVES, CRUSHED

8 OUNCES BABY ZUCCHINI, CUT INTO ¼-INCH ROUNDS

8 OUNCES BABY CARROTS, SLICED IN HALF

1 TEASPOON FINELY CHOPPED FRESH DILL

1 TEASPOON DRIED THYME

DIRECTION

1. Preheat oven to broil. Combine olive oil with garlic in a glass or ceramic baking dish.
2. Add vegetables and mix in dill and thyme.
3. Broil for ten minutes.
4. Stir vegetables, then continue broiling for one minute.
5. Vegetables are done when easily pierced with a fork.
6. Cool for five minutes before serving.

4. NUTTY SUMMER SQUASH

A SIMPLE PREP OF STEAMED SQUASH ACCENTED BY FRESH TOMATOES AND THYME WITH A SNAPPY FINISH OF TOASTED HAZELNUTS TAKES JUST MINUTES TO PREPARE AND IS A COLORFUL ADDITION TO ANY PLATE.

SERVES 4

INGREDIENTS

2 LARGE ZUCCHINI, CUT INTO ½–INCH ROUNDS

2 LARGE YELLOW SQUASH, CUT INTO ½–INCH ROUNDS

2 TABLESPOONS FLAXSEED OIL

1 LARGE HEIRLOOM TOMATO, DICED

1 TABLESPOON MINCED FRESH THYME

2 TABLESPOONS MINCED FRESH PARSLEY

2 TABLESPOONS ROASTED HAZELNUTS

DIRECTION

1. Fill a 2-quart saucepan with 1 quart of water.
2. Insert steamer and bring water to a boil.
3. Add zucchini and yellow squash and cover.
4. Steam ten minutes and stir once.
5. Drain squash and place in medium bowl.
6. Add oil and mix well.
7. Toss with tomatoes and sprinkle with thyme, parsley, and hazelnuts.

5. SUNCHOKE SAUTÉ

SUNCHOKES (BETTER KNOWN AS JERUSALEM ARTICHOKES) ARE A GREAT PART OF THE PALEO DIET. THEY MAKE A DELICIOUS SUBSTITUTE FOR WHITE POTATOES WITHOUT THE NEGATIVE CONSEQUENCES OF A HIGH GLYCEMIC INDEX AND SAPONIN CONTENT.

SERVES 4

INGREDIENTS

2 TABLESPOONS EXTRA VIRGIN OLIVE OIL

2 GARLIC CLOVES, DICED

1 TABLESPOON DRIED OREGANO

1 TABLESPOON MINCED FRESH BASIL

1 TEASPOON DRIED TARRAGON

8 OUNCES SUNCHOKES, PEELED AND CUT INTO ½–INCH SLICES

1 TEASPOON FRESHLY GROUND BLACK PEPPER

4 FRESH PARSLEY SPRIGS

DIRECTION

1. Heat oil in a cast iron skillet over medium heat.
2. Add garlic, oregano, basil, and tarragon and stir for one minute.
3. Add sunchokes and continue to stir for eight to ten minutes, or until tender.
4. Remove from heat and sprinkle with pepper.
5. Garnish with sprigs of parsley.

6. BLASTED VEGGIE MEDLEY

THE SIMPLE ADDITION OF GARLIC AND TEMPTING VIRGIN OLIVE OIL WILL KEEP YOU FROM MISSING THE CHEESE.

SERVES 4

INGREDIENTS

4 TABLESPOONS EXTRA VIRGIN OLIVE OIL

½ SWEET ONION, THINLY SLICED

4 GARLIC CLOVES, FINELY CHOPPED

1 TEASPOON DRIED TARRAGON

1 TEASPOON DRIED OREGANO

1 CUP BROCCOLI FLORETS

1 CUP CAULIFLOWER FLORETS

1 CUP DICED BABY CARROTS LEMON WEDGES, TO TASTE

FRESHLY GROUND PEPPER, TO TASTE

DIRECTION

1. Heat olive oil in a cast iron skillet over medium flame.
2. Add onion, garlic, tarragon, and oregano and sauté while stirring for two to three minutes.
3. Add broccoli, cauliflower, and carrots and continue cooking for three to four minutes.
4. Once the veggies begin to stick to the pan, stir and continue cooking until slightly charred.
5. Turn off heat and cover; let sit for five minutes.
6. Squeeze lemon wedges over veggies, drizzling juice evenly.
7. Sprinkle with freshly ground pepper.

7. Asian Slaw

Make this dish the day before you plan on serving to allow the lemon juice to tenderize the cabbage.

SERVES 4

INGREDIENTS

½ HEAD RED CABBAGE, WASHED AND SHREDDED

1 LARGE CARROT, PEELED AND GRATED

1 TEASPOON GRATED FRESH GINGER JUICE FROM ½ LEMON

2 SCALLIONS, CHOPPED

½ CUP OMEGA 3 MAYONNAISE

¼ CUP DICED DRIED PINEAPPLE

1 TEASPOON WHITE SESAME SEEDS

1 TEASPOON BLACK SESAME SEEDS

DIRECTION

1. Combine the cabbage and carrots in a large flat bowl.
2. Add ginger, lemon juice, scallions, and mayonnaise.
3. Toss thoroughly.
4. Stir in pineapple pieces.
5. Sprinkle with sesame seeds.
6. Cover and refrigerate for twenty-four hours, remixing every few hours.
7. Remove from refrigerator five to ten minutes before serving.

8. CREAM OF BROCCOLI SOUP

ROASTING THE BROCCOLI AND THE ONION ALLOWS THE FLAVORS TO MELLOW AND COMBINE TO PRODUCE A WEALTH OF FLAVOR.

SERVES 4

INGREDIENTS

2 TABLESPOONS EXTRA VIRGIN OLIVE OIL

1 MEDIUM YELLOW ONION, DICED

2 CUPS BROCCOLI FLORETS

1 CUP CHICKEN BROTH

1 TEASPOON FRESHLY SQUEEZED LEMON JUICE

1 TABLESPOON LEMON ZEST

4 TABLESPOONS ROASTED WALNUTS

DIRECTION

1. Preheat oven to broil.
2. Heat oil in a cast iron skillet over medium flame.
3. Add onion and sauté for five to eight minutes, until translucent.
4. Add broccoli and stir until well coated.
5. Place skillet in oven and broil for ten minutes, stirring once.
6. Remove from oven, cover, and let sit for two minutes.
7. Combine broccoli and onion mixture with broth and lemon juice.
8. Puree in a blender until smooth.
9. Pour soup into serving bowls and garnish with lemon zest and walnuts.

9. Brussels Sprouts with Shallots and Pecans

BRUSSELS SPROUTS ARE HIGH IN FIBER, VITAMIN A, POTASSIUM, AND CALCIUM.

SERVES 4

INGREDIENTS

8 OUNCES RAW BRUSSELS SPROUTS

1 OUNCE RAW PECANS, CHOPPED

1 TABLESPOON EXTRA VIRGIN OLIVE OIL

2 SMALL SHALLOTS, MINCED

1 TABLESPOON WALNUT OIL

DIRECTION

1. Remove stem ends of sprouts and cut a crisscross in the bottom of each to ensure even cooking.
2. Fill a 2-quart saucepan with 1 quart of water and bring to a boil.
3. Insert steamer basket, add sprouts, and steam for ten to twelve minutes.
4. Plunge sprouts into a bowl filled with ice water to stop the cooking process.
5. Peel the outer leaves from each sprout and set aside.
6. Chop sprouts and combine with pecans.
7. Heat olive oil in a cast iron skillet over medium flame, adding the chopped sprouts and pecan mixture.
8. Cook and stir for five minutes.
9. Add shallots and stir an additional minute.
10. Just before serving, add the sprout leaves and cook for one minute.
11. Toss thoroughly with walnut oil.

10. CARAMELIZED BROCCOLI WITH ORANGE ZEST

FOR A SWEET TWIST ON THIS VITAMIN-PACKED VEGGIE, WE TOSS BROCCOLI WITH ORANGE JUICE, RESULTING IN A LOVELY CARAMELIZED DISH.

SERVES 4

INGREDIENTS

2-3 BROCCOLI HEADS, CUT INTO BITE-SIZED PIECES

2 TABLESPOONS EXTRA VIRGIN OLIVE OIL

1 TEASPOON FRESHLY GROUND BLACK PEPPER

1 TABLESPOON FRESHLY SQUEEZED ORANGE JUICE

1 TABLESPOON ORANGE ZEST

1 TABLESPOON WALNUT OIL

DIRECTION

1. Preheat oven to broil.
2. Place broccoli in large bowl and toss with olive oil and pepper.
3. Drizzle with orange juice and orange zest and mix thoroughly.
4. Arrange broccoli pieces evenly spaced on a rimmed baking sheet.
5. Broil for ten to twelve minutes, until bright green and slightly tender.
6. Remove from oven and toss with walnut oil.

11. SANDY POINT SPINACH SAUTÉ

SPINACH IS A GREAT SOURCE OF IRON, AND YOU CAN QUADRUPLE ITS ABSORPTION BY COMBINING IT WITH A FOOD HIGH IN VITAMIN C, LIKE RED BELL PEPPERS.

SERVES 4

INGREDIENTS

2 BUNCHES SPINACH

2 TABLESPOONS EXTRA VIRGIN OLIVE OIL

4 GARLIC CLOVES, DICED

1 TABLESPOON FRESH BASIL, MINCED

1 TABLESPOON MINCED FRESH CILANTRO

1 SMALL RED BELL PEPPER, SLICED INTO MATCHSTICKS

1 LEMON, CUT IN HALF

DIRECTION

1. Wash and drain spinach using a salad spinner.
2. Heat oil in a cast iron skillet over medium flame.
3. Stir in garlic for one minute.
4. Toss in the spinach, basil, and cilantro and mix thoroughly for two minutes. Remove from heat.
5. Top with pepper slices.
6. Squeeze half of the lemon over the greens and slice the remaining half to use as a garnish.

12. Dandelion Greens with Lime

A BIT OF JUICE FROM A FRESHLY SQUEEZED LIME AND SOME RED CHILI PEPPER FLAKES ADD EVEN MORE ZING TO THIS TANGY VEGETABLE.

SERVES 4

INGREDIENTS

2 TABLESPOONS EXTRA VIRGIN OLIVE OIL

1 SMALL YELLOW ONION, CHOPPED

1 BUNCH DANDELION GREENS, COARSELY CHOPPED

½ LIME, CUT INTO WEDGES

1 TEASPOON RED CHILI PEPPER FLAKES

DIRECTION

1. Heat oil in a cast iron skillet over medium flame.
2. Add onion, cover, and cook until soft.
3. Add greens and stir, allowing them to cook for two minutes.
4. Just before serving, drizzle with lime juice on top and sprinkle with chili pepper flakes.

13. CARB LOVER'S CAULIFLOWER

HERE'S A FLAVORFUL BUT SIMPLE IDEA TO USE IN LIEU OF THAT HIGH-GLYCEMIC STARCHY VEGETABLE. SERVED WITH A RARE FILET MIGNON AND A FRESH SALAD, THIS DISH WILL SURELY SATISFY THE MEAT-AND-POTATO LOVERS AT YOUR TABLE.

SERVES 4

INGREDIENTS

2 CUPS CAULIFLOWER FLORETS

1 LARGE ZUCCHINI, SLICED INTO 1-INCH ROUNDS

2 TABLESPOONS EXTRA VIRGIN OLIVE OIL

6 GARLIC CLOVES, DICED

½ CUP CHICKEN BROTH

2 TABLESPOONS MINCED FRESH CHIVES FRESHLY GROUND BLACK PEPPER, TO TASTE

DIRECTION

1. Fill a 2-quart pot with 1 inch of water and insert steamer basket.
2. Bring water to a boil.
3. Add cauliflower and steam until tender, about ten minutes.
4. Remove cauliflower and set aside to cool.
5. Add zucchini rounds to pot and steam until soft, about ten minutes.
6. Heat oil in a cast iron skillet over medium flame.
7. Add garlic and cook while stirring for five minutes.
8. Turn off flame and cover.
9. Drain zucchini and let cool for five minutes.
10. When both cauliflower and zucchini are cool, place in blender and add broth.
11. Add garlic and oil mixture. Puree until smooth.
12. Spoon entire mixture back into pot and heat over low flame, stirring occasionally. Sprinkle with chives and pepper to taste.

14. SMOKY SOUTHERN-STYLE COLLARDS

IN LIEU OF FATTY PORK CUTS, DICED LEAN TURKEY SAUTÉED WITH GARLIC AND ONIONS, AND THEN CHARRED, IMPARTS A SAVORY, SMOKY FLAVOR TO THIS DISH WITHOUT THE SATURATED FAT.

SERVES 4

INGREDIENTS

2 TABLESPOONS EXTRA VIRGIN OLIVE OIL

1 MEDIUM YELLOW ONION, DICED

4 GARLIC CLOVES, MINCED

½ TEASPOON DRIED THYME

½ TEASPOON DRIED BASIL

4 OUNCES ROASTED TURKEY BREAST, DICED

2 BUNCHES COLLARD GREENS, COARSELY CHOPPED, WITH STEMS REMOVED

DIRECTION

1. Heat olive oil in a cast iron skillet over medium flame.
2. Stir in onion and sauté for five to eight minutes, until translucent.
3. Add garlic and continue stirring for two to three minutes.
4. Increase heat to high and stir for one minute, lightly charring the onions and garlic. Stir in thyme and basil, reducing flame to medium.
5. Add turkey and cook for two minutes.
6. Toss in collard greens and cook while stirring for two minutes, making sure to mix all ingredients well.

15. EGGPLANT AND BASIL SAUTÉ

WITH JUST A LITTLE OLIVE OIL AND A SLOWER COOKING TIME, EGGPLANT HAS ENOUGH TIME TO SWEAT, WHICH RESULTS IN A SALT-FREE, TENDER DISH.

SERVES 4

INGREDIENTS

2 TABLESPOONS EXTRA VIRGIN OLIVE OIL

2 GARLIC CLOVES, MINCED

1 LARGE EGGPLANT, CUT INTO ½-INCH SLICES AFTER STEMS HAVE BEEN REMOVED

4 LARGE FRESH BASIL LEAVES, COARSELY CHOPPED

2 TABLESPOONS DRIED OREGANO

DIRECTION

1. Heat oil and garlic in a cast iron skillet over medium flame and stir for one minute. Add eggplant slices.
2. Cover and turn every five minutes for twenty minutes. (The eggplant may stick slightly at first; just keep cooking and turning.)
3. Sprinkle with basil and oregano, cover, and continue cooking for five minutes. Remove from heat and let stand for five minutes before serving.

16. BRAISED LEEKS WITH GARLIC

THE ADDITION OF SHALLOT, WHITE WINE, AND A HINT OF GARLIC TURNS THIS DISH INTO THE PERFECT ACCOMPANIMENT FOR A PALEO MAIN COURSE.

SERVES 4

INGREDIENTS

2 TABLESPOONS EXTRA VIRGIN OLIVE OIL

1 MEDIUM SHALLOT, DICED

2 GARLIC CLOVES, MINCED

2 LARGE LEEKS, ROOTS AND TOP GREEN PORTIONS REMOVED

½ CUP DRY WHITE WINE OR CHICKEN BROTH FRESHLY GROUND BLACK PEPPER, TO

TASTE

DIRECTION

1. Preheat oven to 200 degrees.
2. Heat olive oil and shallot in a covered cast iron skillet over medium flame for one minute.
3. Stir in garlic and continue cooking for one minute.
4. Move the garlic and shallot to the sides of the pan to make room for the leeks in the center.
5. Cut leek stems in half lengthwise and place in pan cut side down.
6. Cover and cook for two minutes, turning once.
7. Remove from heat and turn leeks cut side up.
8. Spread shallot and garlic evenly on top of leeks.
9. Add wine or chicken broth to pan.
10. Cover with foil, place in oven, and steam for forty-five minutes.
11. Leeks are done when tender and fragrant.
12. Remove from oven and cool for five minutes.
13. Cut leeks in half widthwise before serving.
14. Sprinkle with freshly ground pepper.

17. FLAX-DUSTED LEAFY GREENS

DON'T HESITATE TO TRY ALL SORTS OF LEAFY GREEN VEGETABLES: SPINACH, MUSTARD GREENS, DANDELION GREENS, OR BEET GREENS.

SERVES 4

INGREDIENTS

2 BUNCHES RAINBOW CHARD OR KALE, OR ANY COMBINATION OF GREENS

2 TABLESPOONS EXTRA VIRGIN OLIVE OIL

2 TABLESPOONS FRESHLY GROUND FLAXSEED

DIRECTION

1. Remove stems from greens and finely chop. Set aside.
2. Coarsely chop the leaves and set aside.
3. Heat oil in a cast iron skillet over medium flame.
4. Add chopped stems and sauté for two to three minutes.
5. Turn off heat and cover.
6. Before serving, turn the flame to medium, and add leaves, stirring for one to two minutes.
7. Sprinkle with ground flaxseed.

18. WILD ROASTED MUSHROOMS

MOST MUSHROOMS ARE PREPARED WITH COPIOUS AMOUNTS OF BUTTER OR MARGARINE.

SERVES 4

INGREDIENTS

4 TABLESPOONS EXTRA VIRGIN OLIVE OIL

2 GARLIC CLOVES, DICED

8 OUNCES CREMINI MUSHROOMS, COARSELY CHOPPED

8 OUNCES OYSTER MUSHROOMS, COARSELY CHOPPED

3.5 OUNCES ENOKI MUSHROOMS, COARSELY CHOPPED

1 TABLESPOON DRIED BASIL

1 TEASPOON DRIED TARRAGON

1 TEASPOON PAPRIKA

2 TABLESPOONS CHOPPED FRESH PARSLEY

DIRECTION

1. Preheat oven to broil.
2. Combine olive oil and garlic in a baking dish.
3. Add mushrooms and sprinkle with basil, tarragon, paprika, and parsley.
4. Broil for thirty minutes, stirring mixture at the halfway point.
5. Remove from oven and cool for five minutes.

19. BRAISED CHARD

*LUSH GREEN CHARD LEAVES AND COLORFUL STEMS ARE PUNCHED UP WITH
BROWNED GARLIC AND FIERY CRUSHED RED PEPPER FLAKES.*

SERVES 4

INGREDIENTS

1 LB. (450G) SWISS CHARD

1 TB. EXTRA-VIRGIN OLIVE OIL

2 GARLIC CLOVES, THINLY SLICED

1 TSP. CRUSHED RED PEPPER FLAKES

1/4 TSP. SEA SALT

DIRECTION

1. Using a knife, carefully separate Swiss chard stems from leaves.
2. Coarsely chop leaves and finely slice stems.
3. Heat a large skillet over medium- high heat. When the skillet is hot, add extra-virgin olive oil and wait 30 seconds.
4. Add garlic and Swiss chard stems, and sauté, stirring frequently, for 30 seconds to 1 minute, or until garlic is very aromatic and beginning to turn golden brown.
5. Add Swiss chard leaves, crushed red pepper flakes, and sea salt.
6. Continue to sauté, stirring frequently, for 1 minute, or until leaves wilt.
7. Remove from heat and serve immediately.

20. Eggplant à la Française (Ratatouille)

This veggie dish takes only minutes to prepare, which makes it an ideal recipe for the busy cook. Bon appetit.

SERVES 4

INGREDIENTS

4 TABLESPOONS EXTRA VIRGIN OLIVE OIL

1 MEDIUM YELLOW ONION, CHOPPED

2 GARLIC CLOVES, MINCED

2 LARGE ZUCCHINI, CUT INTO 2 × ½ INCH STRIPS

1 GREEN BELL PEPPER, CUT INTO 2 × ½ INCH STRIPS

1 YELLOW BELL PEPPER, CUT INTO 2 × ½ INCH STRIPS

1 MEDIUM EGGPLANT, CUT INTO 2 × ½ INCH STRIPS

2 PLUM TOMATOES, SEEDED AND CHOPPED

1 BAY LEAF FRESH PARSLEY, TO TASTE

DIRECTION

1. Heat 2 tablespoons of the olive oil in a cast iron skillet over medium flame.
2. Add chopped onion and sauté for five minutes.
3. Toss in garlic and continue to sauté for one minute.
4. Place zucchini in skillet, stirring occasionally for five minutes.
5. Pour into a bowl and set aside.
6. Add another tablespoon of the olive oil and bell peppers to skillet.
7. Sauté for five minutes, stirring occasionally.
8. Brush the last tablespoon of olive oil evenly over eggplant and place in skillet.
9. Cook for five minutes, stirring occasionally.
10. Place zucchini and peppers back in skillet with the eggplant.
11. Mix in tomato, bay leaf, and parsley.
12. Cover and cook for ten minutes. May be served warm or cold.

21. RAVING RAPINI

FOR THOSE WHO ARE LEARNING TO ENJOY NEW VEGGIES AND WANT SOMETHING FAMILIAR IN THE MIX, RAISINS OFFER A BIT OF SWEET TO BALANCE THE TASTE.

SERVES 4

INGREDIENTS

1 BUNCH RAPINI (BROCCOLI RABE)

1 LEMON

1 TEASPOON DRIED DILL

1 TEASPOON BASIL

2 TABLESPOONS COLD-PRESSED FLAXSEED OIL

¼ CUP SUN-DRIED TOMATOES

2 TABLESPOONS RAISINS

DIRECTION

1. Coarsely chop rapini and place in a cast iron skillet with 1 inch water.
2. Steam for about five minutes until bright green, stirring once or twice to ensure even cooking.
3. Drain and cool for five minutes.
4. Squeeze half of the lemon into a small jar.
5. Add dill, basil, and flaxseed oil.
6. Cover and shake.
7. Toss into rapini, then add sun-dried tomatoes and raisins.
8. Cut the other half of the lemon into wedges for a garnish.

22. ROASTY TOASTY BEETS WITH HAZELNUTS

ROASTING THIS ROOT VEGETABLE BRINGS OUT ITS FLAVOR, WHICH IS FURTHER ENHANCED BY THE DELECTABLE HAZELNUT FINISH.

SERVES 4

INGREDIENTS

1 BUNCH BEETS, LEAVES REMOVED AND BEETS QUARTERED

2 TABLESPOONS EXTRA VIRGIN OLIVE OIL

1 TABLESPOON DRIED BASIL

1 GARLIC CLOVE, PRESSED

2 TABLESPOONS CHOPPED ROASTED HAZELNUTS (FILBERTS) FRESHLY GROUND BLACK
PEPPER, TO TASTE

DIRECTION

1. Preheat oven to broil.
2. Toss beets with olive oil, basil, and garlic in a glass or ceramic baking dish.
3. Broil for thirty minutes, stirring once at the halfway point.
4. Top with roasted hazelnuts and pepper.

23. RAW KALE FUSION

THIS DISH IS BEST PREPARED THE DAY BEFORE SERVING TO ALLOW THE KALE TO MARINATE AND SOFTEN.

SERVES 4

INGREDIENTS

1 HEAD RED KALE, COARSELY CHOPPED, WITH STEMS REMOVED

1 HEAD GREEN KALE, COARSELY CHOPPED, WITH STEMS REMOVED

½ SMALL RED ONION

2 GARLIC CLOVES

2 TABLESPOONS EXTRA VIRGIN OLIVE OIL

2 TABLESPOONS COLD–PRESSED FLAXSEED OIL JUICE FROM 1 LIME

FRESHLY GROUND BLACK PEPPER, TO TASTE

1 FRESH HEIRLOOM OR BEEFSTEAK TOMATO

2 ORANGE SLICES

DIRECTION

1. Place kale in a wide shallow bowl.
2. Combine red onion and garlic in a small food processor and pulse until finely chopped.
3. Add garlic and onion mixture to kale.
4. Toss in oils and lime juice and mix thoroughly.
5. Sprinkle with freshly ground pepper.
6. Cover with plastic wrap and refrigerate; stir two or three times over the next twenty-four hours.
7. Just before serving, chop the tomato and add it to the kale mixture.
8. Garnish with orange slices.

24. BACK-TO-OUR-ROOTS WINTER VEGGIES

PALEO-FRIENDLY WINTER DISH, WITH HEARTY AND SAVORY FLAVORS TO WARM UP COLD WINTER NIGHTS.

SERVES 4

INGREDIENTS

2 MEDIUM TURNIPS, PEELED AND CUT INTO ½–INCH PIECES

2 MEDIUM PARSNIPS, PEELED AND CUT INTO ½–INCH PIECES

1 MEDIUM RUTABAGA, PEELED AND CUT INTO ½–INCH PIECES 1 MEDIUM YAM, CUT INTO ½–INCH PIECES

1 MEDIUM YELLOW ONION, CHOPPED 2 TABLESPOONS EXTRA VIRGIN OLIVE OIL

1 WHOLE GARLIC BULB

1 SPRIG FRESH ROSEMARY, STEM REMOVED FRESHLY GROUND BLACK PEPPER, TO TASTE

DIRECTION

1. Preheat oven to 400 degrees.
2. Spread turnips, parsnips, rutabaga, yam, and onion evenly on a large rimmed baking sheet and drizzle with oil.
3. Wrap garlic bulb in foil and place in middle of baking sheet.
4. Scatter rosemary leaves over the veggies.
5. Bake for one hour and stir occasionally to ensure even cooking.
6. Remove from oven.
7. Remove foil from garlic and place in center of serving dish.
8. Arrange veggies around the garlic.
9. Sprinkle with freshly ground black pepper.
10. Garlic can be easily pressed from skin for a tasty addition.

25. Baked Holiday Stuffing

This Paleo recipe is a truly fantastic alternative to traditional stuffing. Enjoy and celebrate!

SERVES 4

INGREDIENTS

2 TABLESPOONS EXTRA VIRGIN OLIVE OIL

4 LARGE CELERY STALKS, DICED

1 MEDIUM YELLOW ONION, DICED

4 PORTOBELLO MUSHROOMS, COARSELY CHOPPED

1 MEDIUM SHALLOT, MINCED

½ CUP CHICKEN BROTH

2 TABLESPOONS FRESHLY GROUND FLAXSEED

2 TABLESPOONS MINCED FRESH SAGE

4 OUNCES BRAZIL NUTS, TOASTED AND COARSELY CHOPPED

DIRECTION

1. Preheat oven to 350 degrees.
2. Heat olive oil in a cast iron skillet over medium flame.
3. Add celery, onions, and mushrooms and stir occasionally for ten minutes.
4. Toss in shallot and continue cooking for two minutes.
5. Pour in broth and stir.
6. Remove from heat.
7. Stir in flaxseed, sage, and Brazil nuts.
8. Bake for twenty minutes.

26. TOKYO SESAME WAKAME

SEAWEED IS THE PERFECT SIDE DISH TO PAIR WITH THIS JAPANESE DELICACY. THIS PALEO RECIPE IS HEALTHY AND DELICIOUS.

SERVES 4

INGREDIENTS

2 OUNCES WAKAME (PURCHASE A BRAND THAT IS ENTIRELY SEAWEED WITH NO ADDITIVES)

2 TABLESPOONS COLD-PRESSED FLAXSEED OIL

2 LARGE CARROTS, GRATED

2 SCALLIONS, FINELY CHOPPED

1 TABLESPOON FRESHLY SQUEEZED LEMON JUICE

½ TEASPOON BLACK SESAME SEEDS

½ TEASPOON WHITE SESAME SEEDS

DIRECTION

1. Put the dried seaweed in 2 cups of water and let sit for ten minutes, then drain.
2. Add the flaxseed oil, carrots, scallions, and lemon juice.
3. Toss and sprinkle with black and white sesame seeds.

27. SAUTÉED GREEN BEANS WITH LAMB BACON

THIS RECIPE USES LAMB BACON TO FLAVOR THE BEANS. TRADITIONAL MEDITERRANEAN COOKING USES A VARIETY OF ANIMAL FATS, WHICH INFUSE RICH FLAVORS INTO THE VEGETABLES.

SERVES 4

INGREDIENTS

1 POUND GREEN BEANS, TRIMMED

FINE SEA SALT AND GROUND BLACK PEPPER

4 OUNCES LAMB BACON OR BACON OF CHOICE

2 TEASPOONS MINCED GARLIC

1 TEASPOON PAPRIKA

DIRECTION

1. Heat a steamer pot with 3 cups of water over medium heat.
2. Place the green beans in the top with a pinch of salt and cover.
3. Steam them for 5 minutes, or until slightly cooked.
4. Chop the lamb bacon into small pieces.
5. Heat a skillet over medium heat.
6. Add the bacon pieces and garlic to a skillet and cook for 5 minutes.
7. Add the green beans and paprika and stir.
8. Sauté the mixture for 3 minutes to combine the flavors.
9. Add salt and pepper to taste and serve.

LAMB BACON CAN BE FOUND AT SPECIALTY BUTCHER SHOPS OR HALAL OR KOSHER STORES. REGULAR BACON CAN BE USED IF DESIRED.

28. PERFECT SWEET POTATO FRIES

Avoid polyunsaturated oils, such as canola, corn, and soybean oils. They are heavily processed, making them oxidized before they reach your table.

SERVES 4

INGREDIENTS

4 LARGE SWEET POTATOES

2 CUPS SUSTAINABLE PALM SHORTENING, COCONUT OIL, OR BEEF TALLOW

FINE SEA SALT TO TASTE

PAPRIKA TO TASTE

DIRECTION

1. Peel the sweet potatoes and cut them lengthwise into thin strips.
2. In a deep skillet, heat the fat over medium-high heat until hot. To check the temperature, insert the end of a wooden spoon handle into the fat; if bubbles form all around it, the oil is ready to use.
3. Add the sweet potatoes, making sure they don't clump together, and cover.
4. Cook for 5 to 7 minutes, until golden brown.
5. Transfer the fries to a paper towel to drain.
6. Sprinkle with salt and paprika and serve immediately.

29. SAVORY SWEET POTATO CAKES

SWEET POTATOES ARE HIGH IN BETA-CAROTENE, AN ANTIOXIDANT, AND SHOULD BE EATEN WITH FATS SUCH AS OLIVE OIL OR GRASS-FED BUTTER TO INCREASE ITS ABSORPTION.

SERVES 6 CAKES

INGREDIENTS

4 MEDIUM SWEET POTATOES

1/2 CUP COCONUT FLOUR

1 TEASPOON PAPRIKA

2 TEASPOONS GROUND CUMIN

1 TEASPOON CAYENNE PEPPER

FINE SEA SALT AND GROUND BLACK PEPPER

2 LARGE EGGS, BEATEN

1/2 CUP CHOPPED FRESH CILANTRO, PLUS MORE FOR GARNISH

1/4 CUP SUSTAINABLE PALM SHORTENING, COCONUT OIL, OR BEEF TALLOW

DIRECTION

1. Preheat the oven to 350°F.
2. Bake the sweet potatoes for 1 hour, or until easily pierced with a knife. Allow to cool, then remove and discard the skin.
3. Place the cooked sweet potatoes in a large bowl.
4. In a small bowl, use a fork to mix together the coconut flour, paprika, cumin, cayenne pepper, a pinch of salt and pepper, the eggs, and the cilantro.
5. Pour the egg mixture into the bowl with the sweet potatoes and mix well. Form the sweet potatoes into 6 evenly sized patties.
6. Melt the fat in a skillet over medium heat.
7. Add the patties and cook for 3 to 4 minutes on each side, until golden brown. The cakes will be crispy on the outside and soft in the middle when done.
8. Garnish with the cilantro to serve.

30. WARM EGGPLANT AND TOMATO SALAD WITH MINT (ZAALOUK)

EGGPLANT IS A VERSATILE VEGETABLE THAT EASILY ABSORBS OTHER FLAVORS AND CAN BE USED IN MAIN DISHES AND SIDES. IT WORKS WELL AS A STUFFING OR THICKENER IN MANY DISHES, SUCH AS MOUSSAKA.

SERVES 4

INGREDIENTS

1 TABLESPOON UNSALTED BUTTER, COCONUT OIL, OR GHEE

1 MEDIUM WHITE ONION, DICED

1 TABLESPOON MINCED GARLIC

3 ROMA TOMATOES, CHOPPED

FINE SEA SALT AND GROUND BLACK PEPPER

1 LARGE EGGPLANT

2 MEDIUM ZUCCHINI

1 TEASPOON GROUND CUMIN 1 TEASPOON CHILI POWDER

1/2 CUP CHOPPED FRESH PARSLEY

1 TABLESPOON APPLE CIDER VINEGAR

1/4 CUP EXTRA-VIRGIN OLIVE OIL, FOR GARNISH

1/4 CUP CHOPPED FRESH MINT LEAVES, FOR GARNISH

DIRECTION

1. Melt the fat in a skillet over medium heat.
2. Add the onion, garlic, and tomatoes with a few pinches of salt and pepper. Sauté the onion mixture for 10 minutes.
3. While the onion and tomatoes are cooking, dice the eggplant and zucchini into bite-sized pieces. Add the eggplant, zucchini, cumin, chili powder, and parsley to the skillet. Sauté the mixture for 10 to 15 more minutes, or until the vegetables are well cooked.
4. Add the vinegar to the pan and stir.
5. Garnish the dish with the olive oil and mint leaves.

31. MOCK POTATO SALAD

TO MAKE SURE YOUR TURNIPS ARE VERY FRESH, CHECK THAT THE GREENS ON THE TOP LOOK VIBRANT. A GOOD TRICK TO REDUCE THE BITTERNESS OF TURNIPS IS TO BOIL A POTATO IN THE WATER WITH THE TURNIPS.

SERVES 4

INGREDIENTS

6 TO 8 MEDIUM TURNIPS (ABOUT 2 POUNDS), PEELED AND CUT INTO BITE-SIZED PIECES

FINE SEA SALT AND GROUND BLACK PEPPER

1/4 CUP AIOLI

1 TEASPOON DRY MUSTARD

2 TABLESPOONS APPLE CIDER VINEGAR

1/2 CUP FRESH CILANTRO LEAVES, CHOPPED

1 MEDIUM RED ONION, MINCED (OPTIONAL)

DIRECTION

1. Place the turnips in a stockpot, cover with water, and bring to a boil.
2. Boil the turnips until fork-tender, about 20 minutes.
3. Transfer the turnips to a bowl and let cool for 5 minutes.
4. Make the dressing: In a small bowl, mix together a pinch of salt and pepper and the aioli, dry mustard, vinegar, and cilantro.
5. Add the red onion, if using, to the bowl of turnips. Add the dressing and toss well to coat.
6. Serve warm or chilled.

32. ROASTED EGGPLANT CASSEROLE

OMIT THE GARLIC. USE GARLIC-INFUSED OLIVE OIL IN PLACE OF THE OLIVE OIL. OMIT THE CHEESE. USE 1/2 CUP CHOPPED TOMATOES IN PLACE OF THE TOMATO PASTE.

SERVES 4

INGREDIENTS

1 TABLESPOON UNSALTED BUTTER, GHEE, OR COCONUT OIL, FOR GREASING THE DISH

2 LARGE EGGPLANTS

4 CLOVES GARLIC, PEELED

1/4 CUP EXTRA–VIRGIN OLIVE OIL

1 TEASPOON DRIED THYME LEAVES

1 TABLESPOON TOMATO PASTE

2 LARGE EGGS, BEATEN

2 TABLESPOONS GRATED PARMESAN CHEESE (OPTIONAL)

DIRECTION

1. Preheat the oven to 350°F. Grease a 2-quart casserole dish or 8-inch-square glass baking dish.
2. Poke 2 holes in each eggplant with a knife and stuff in the garlic cloves.
3. Place the eggplants in the prepared baking dish.
4. Roast the eggplants for 30 minutes, or until soft. Let them cool and remove the skin. (Do not wash the baking dish; you will use it again.)
5. In a large bowl, mash the eggplant flesh with a fork.
6. Add the olive oil, thyme, tomato paste, and eggs and stir until well combined.
7. Pour the mixture into the baking dish.
8. Bake for 20 minutes, or until cooked through.
9. If using the cheese, turn the oven to broil.
10. Remove the dish and sprinkle the cheese over the top.
11. Return it to the oven and broil for 2 minutes, or until browned.

33. GOLDEN RAISIN SLAW

FOLLOW THIS HEALTHIER VERSION WITH MEDITERRANEAN FLAVORS AND NO PROCESSED OILS.

SERVES 4

INGREDIENTS

1 MEDIUM HEAD CABBAGE, SHREDDED

2 MEDIUM CARROTS, SHREDDED

1 CUP GOLDEN RAISINS

1/4 CUP EXTRA-VIRGIN OLIVE OIL

1/4 CUP LEMON JUICE

2 TABLESPOONS FINELY CHOPPED FRESH MINT

2 TABLESPOONS FINELY CHOPPED FRESH CILANTRO

1 TEASPOON HERBES DE PROVENCE

FINE SEA SALT AND GROUND BLACK PEPPER TO TASTE

DIRECTION

1. Place all the ingredients in a large bowl and toss until well combined.
2. Adjust the seasonings to taste.
3. Let the salad chill for 1 hour in the refrigerator before serving.

34. CAULIFLOWER COUSCOUS

IF MAKING RAISIN AND PINE NUT COUSCOUS, OMIT THE PINE NUTS OR USE PUMPKIN SEEDS IN THEIR PLACE.

SERVES 4

INGREDIENTS

1 LARGE HEAD CAULIFLOWER, CORED

FINE SEA SALT AND GROUND BLACK PEPPER

1/4 CUP CHOPPED FRESH CILANTRO

DIRECTION

1. Rinse the cauliflower and let it drain. Cut the cauliflower into florets.
2. Use a food processor with a shredder blade to shred the florets.
3. Put the shredded cauliflower in a steamer pot with 3 cups of water over medium heat.
4. Season with a few pinches of salt and pepper and steam for 5 to 8 minutes, until cooked but still firm to the bite, not mushy.
5. Place the cauliflower in a large bowl.
6. Add the cilantro and stir to combine.

RAISIN AND PINE NUT COUSCOUS

To the cooked and still-warm cauliflower, add 1/2 cup raisins and 1/2 cup pine nuts and toss for a sweet and crunchy change of pace. Top with the fresh cilantro.

SAFFRON COUSCOUS

Steep 1/2 teaspoon saffron threads and 1 teaspoon turmeric in 2 tablespoons of boiling water. Pour the spiced water over the cooked and still-warm cauliflower and toss until well combined. Top with the fresh cilantro.

35. CHERMOULA ROASTED VEGETABLES

ROASTED ROOT VEGETABLES HAVE ALWAYS BEEN A FAVORITE OF OURS BECAUSE OVEN-ROASTING BRINGS OUT THE SWEETNESS IN THE VEGETABLES. THIS DISH ADDS CHERMOULA, A MARINADE USED IN ALGERIAN, MOROCCAN, AND TUNISIAN COOKING. THERE ARE MANY DIFFERENT REGIONAL VARIATIONS, AND OTHER SEASONINGS CAN INCLUDE LEMON, CUMIN, CHILI PEPPER, SAFFRON, AND ONION. THESE SPICED VEGETABLES PAIR WELL WITH LAMB-STUFFED CHICKEN THIGHS.

SERVES 4

INGREDIENTS

1 TABLESPOON COCONUT OIL, FOR GREASING THE PAN

3 MEDIUM TURNIPS, PEELED AND CUT INTO BITE–SIZED PIECES

3 LARGE CARROTS, PEELED AND CUT INTO BITE–SIZED PIECES

2 STALKS CELERY, DICED

1 MEDIUM FENNEL BULB, DICED

2 TEASPOONS MINCED GARLIC

1 TABLESPOON GROUND CUMIN 1 TEASPOON PAPRIKA

1 TEASPOON CAYENNE PEPPER

3 CUPS TIGHTLY PACKED FRESH CILANTRO LEAVES

FINE SEA SALT AND GROUND BLACK PEPPER

2 TABLESPOONS LEMON JUICE

1/2 CUP EXTRA–VIRGIN OLIVE OIL

DIRECTION

1. Preheat the oven to 350°F. Grease a rimmed sheet pan or glass baking dish.

2. In a large bowl, combine the turnips, carrots, celery, and fennel.

3. Put the garlic, cumin, paprika, cayenne pepper, cilantro, a pinch of salt and pepper, the lemon juice, and the olive oil in a food processor and pulse until smooth.

4. Pour the sauce over the vegetables and toss until they are fully coated. Let the vegetables marinate at room temperature for about 15 minutes.

5. Pour the vegetables into the prepared pan and spread them out evenly. Bake the vegetable mixture for 25 to 30 minutes, until tender.

36. MARINATED OLIVES

MAKE SURE THE ONLY ADDITIVES TO THE OLIVES ARE SALT AND WATER. OMIT THE TOMATOES AND USE 1 TEASPOON GROUND GINGER IN PLACE OF THE PAPRIKA. THIS RECIPE SPICES THEM UP FOR A TASTY APPETIZER OR SIDE DISH.

SERVES 6 TO 8

INGREDIENTS

2 POUNDS UNPITTED GREEN OLIVES

1/2 CUP DICED RED ONION

3 TABLESPOONS MINCED GARLIC

1 CUP EXTRA-VIRGIN OLIVE OIL

2 BAY LEAVES, CRUSHED

2 TEASPOONS FINELY GRATED LEMON ZEST

1 LEMON, THINLY SLICED

1 CUP DICED SUNDRIED TOMATOES

1 TEASPOON PAPRIKA

1/2 CUP FRESH CILANTRO, CHOPPED

DIRECTION

1. Rinse the olives in cool water and drain.
2. Place them in a large bowl.
3. Add the rest of the ingredients to the bowl.
4. Stir until well mixed and refrigerate for up to 8 hours.

37. FERMENTED PROBIOTIC PICKLES

NATURALLY FERMENTED FOODS ARE ONE OF THE FEW SOURCES OF VITAMIN K2, WHICH IS IMPORTANT FOR BONE HEALTH. NATURALLY FERMENTED FOODS ALSO PROVIDE BENEFICIAL BACTERIA FOR THE COLON, WHICH CAN BECOME OUT OF BALANCE FROM ANTIBIOTICS AND A TYPICAL AMERICAN DIET. PICKLING DOES NOT PROVIDE THE SAME PROBIOTIC BENEFITS AS FERMENTING.

SERVES 4

INGREDIENTS

5 TO 7 PERSIAN CUCUMBERS

2 TABLESPOONS FINE SEA SALT

1 TABLESPOON CUMIN SEEDS

1 TABLESPOON MINCED GARLIC

2 SPRIGS FRESH DILL

1 CUP TIGHTLY PACKED FRESH CILANTRO LEAVES

1 GRAPE OR CABBAGE LEAF

DIRECTION

1. Rinse the cucumbers and put them in a 2-quart jar.
2. In a medium bowl, mix the salt with 4 cups of water until the salt dissolves.
3. Pour the salt water into the jar with the cucumbers.
4. Add the cumin seeds, garlic, dill, and cilantro to the jar and stir slightly.
5. Add the grape leaf and push the cucumbers down until they are covered with brine.
6. Seal the jar and leave at room temperature. Pickles will ferment in 1 to 2 weeks. Periodically check to make sure the cucumbers are still submerged under the brine. If they're sticking out of the brine, just push them back down or add a little water until water and the grape leaf cover them.
7. Monitor the cucumbers for desired taste and texture. After sitting for about 2 weeks, they will be ready to eat. Store in the fridge to slow the fermentation.
8. Enjoy as a side dish or a snack.

38. ROASTED CARROTS WITH CUMIN AND YOGURT

THIS SIMPLE SIDE IS AN ABSOLUTE SHOWSTOPPER WHEN YOU USE PURPLE, ORANGE, YELLOW, AND RED CARROTS.

THESE GORGEOUS RAINBOW CARROTS CAN OFTEN BE FOUND YEAR-ROUND AT MOST HIGH-END MARKETS.

SERVES 4

INGREDIENTS

1 LB. (450G) SMALL CARROTS, TRIMMED AND HALVED LENGTHWISE

2 TB. EXTRA-VIRGIN OLIVE OIL

1 TSP. RAW HONEY

1/2 TSP. SEA SALT

1/2 TSP. FRESHLY GROUND BLACK PEPPER

1 TSP. WHOLE CUMIN SEEDS

1/2 MEDIUM LEMON, CUT INTO 4 WEDGES

1/4 CUP FULL-FAT YOGURT OR FULL-FAT COCONUT CREAM (OPTIONAL)

DIRECTION

1. Preheat the oven to 425°F (220°C).
2. In a medium bowl, toss carrots in extra-virgin olive oil and raw honey.
3. Spread carrots evenly over a metal baking sheet.
4. Sprinkle with sea salt, black pepper, and
5. cumin seeds.
6. Bake for 25 to 30 minutes, or until tender.
7. Squeeze fresh lemon juice over top and serve alongside full-fat yogurt for dipping.

39. ROMANESCO WITH PINE NUTS

ROMANESCO IS A GORGEOUS BRASSICA, CLOSELY RELATED TO BOTH BROCCOLI AND CAULIFLOWER. IT'S QUITE DISTINCT, DUE TO THE GEOMETRIC PATTERN THAT LOOKS LIKE A FRACTAL.

SERVES 4

INGREDIENTS

V 2 LB. (680G) ROMANESCO, CUT INTO SMALL BOWL

2 TB. TOASTED PINE NUTS

V 4 TSP. COARSE SEA SALT

1 TB. FRESH LEMON JUICE

DIRECTION

1. Medium-high heat. When the skillet is hot, add extra-virgin olive oil and wait 30 seconds.

2. Stirring, for 2 to 3 minutes, or until deep golden brown on one side.

3. Stir carefully and turn heat down to low.

4. Hand lemon juice on top.

5. Cover and steam for 2 to 3 minutes, or until Romanesco is tender.

40. ROMANESCO WITH PINE NUTS AND SAFFRON ALIOLI

WHILE ITS TEXTURE IS SIMILAR TO CAULIFLOWER, THE TASTE IS SLIGHTLY NUTTIER THAN ITS TRADITIONAL COUNTERPART.

SERVES 4

INGREDIENTS

6 TO 8 SAFFRON THREADS 1 TSP. WARM WATER

1 LARGE GARLIC CLOVE, PRESSED OR VERY fiNELY MINCED

1⁄4 TSP. SEA SALT

1⁄4 TSP. DIJON MUSTARD

1 LARGE EGG YOLK, AT ROOM TEMPERATURE

3⁄4 CUP EXTRA-VIRGIN OLIVE OIL, AT ROOM TEMPERATURE

1 TB. FRESH LEMON JUICE

DIRECTION

1. Place saffron threads in 1 teaspoon warm water and let sit for 5 minutes.
2. Using the broad side of a knife, scrape garlic clove with sea salt until a fine paste forms. Alternately, use a mortar and pestle or a press to mash garlic into a smooth paste with no remaining chunks.
3. Place garlic paste, Dijon mustard, saffron threads (with residual water), and egg yolk into a wide-mouth pint-size Mason jar. Using an immersion blender, pulse mixture for 15 seconds, or until fully blended.
4. Add 2 drops extra-virgin olive oil and blend for 10 seconds. Add 2 more drops extra-virgin olive oil and blend for 10 seconds.
5. Continue adding oil 1 teaspoon at a time and blending at 10-second intervals until a
6. mayonnaise consistency begins to form. At that point, pour in remaining extra-virgin olive oil and blend until fully incorporated.
7. Add lemon juice and blend until combined. Taste and adjust salt or lemon as needed.
8. Serve with Romanesco with Pine Nuts.

41. ROASTED RADICCHIO WITH CHERMOULA AND WALNUTS

CHERMOULA IS TRADITIONALLY USED AS A TOPPING FOR FISH OR SEAFOOD, BUT IS JUST AS TASTY ON VEGETABLES, CHICKEN, OR LAMB.

SERVES 4

INGREDIENTS

1/2 CUPS CILANTRO

1/2 CUP AT-LEAF PARSLEY

6 GARLIC CLOVES, SLICED

1 TSP. GROUND CUMIN 1 TSP. SMOKED PAPRIKA

3/4 TSP. SEA SALT

1/4 TSP. CAYENNE PEPPER

1/2 CUP EXTRA-VIRGIN OLIVE OIL

2 TB. FRESH LEMON JUICE

3 HEADS RADICCHIO, QUARTERED

1/2 CUP WALNUTS, CHOPPED

DIRECTION

1. Preheat the oven to 400°F (200°C).
2. To make chermoula, combine cilantro, flat-leaf parsley, garlic, cumin, smoked paprika, sea salt, cayenne pepper, extra-virgin olive oil, and lemon juice in a food processor.
3. Pulse for 30 seconds, or until a paste forms. Taste and adjust seasonings, if desired. Toss radicchio quarters in just enough chermoula to coat.
4. Spread radicchio on a rimmed baking sheet.
5. Bake for 12 to 15 minutes, turning once, until wilted and tender.
6. Meanwhile, place walnuts in a small skillet over low heat.
7. Toast, stirring frequently, for 3 to 4 minutes, or until aromatic.
8. Remove from the skillet immediately.
9. To serve, top roasted radicchio with toasted walnuts.

42. CELERY ROOTS "PATATAS" BRAVAS

EACH SERVING HAS:

> *CALORIES 150*
>
> *TOTAL FAT 7G*
>
> *CARBOHYDRATE 19G*
>
> *PROTEIN 0G*

SERVES 4

INGREDIENTS

3 LARGE CELERY ROOTS, TRIMMED AND PEELED

3 TB. EXTRA–VIRGIN OLIVE OIL

1 TSP. SEA SALT

2 TSP. SMOKED PAPRIKA

1 TSP. CAYENNE PEPPER (USE LESS OR MORE AS PREFERRED)

DIRECTION

1. Preheat the oven to 350°F (180°C).
2. Chop celery roots into 1-inch (2.5cm) cubes. Toss cubes with extra-virgin olive oil, sea salt, smoked paprika, and cayenne pepper.
3. Cut a piece of parchment paper to line the bottom of a large rimmed baking sheet (or use a silicone sheet liner).
4. Spread seasoned celery roots evenly over the baking sheet.
5. Bake for 20 to 30 minutes, stirring every 10 minutes, until firm but tender when pierced with a fork. Serve warm with a side of Alioli.

43. ALIOLI

ADD LEMON JUICE AND BLEND UNTIL COMBINED. TASTE AND ADJUST SALT OR LEMON JUICE AS NEEDED BEFORE SERVING WITH CELERY ROOT "PATATAS."

SERVES 4

INGREDIENTS

1 LARGE GARLIC CLOVE, PRESSED OR MINCED

1⁄4 TSP. SEA SALT

1⁄4 TSP. DIJON MUSTARD

1 LARGE EGG YOLK, AT ROOM TEMPERATURE

3⁄4 CUP EXTRA-VIRGIN OLIVE OIL, AT ROOM TEMPERATURE

1 TB. FRESH LEMON JUICE

DIRECTION

1. Using the broad side of a knife, scrape garlic clove with sea salt until a fine paste forms. Alternately, use a mortar and pestle or a press to mash garlic into a smooth paste.

2. Place garlic paste, Dijon mustard, and egg yolk into a wide-mouth pint-size Mason jar.

3. Using an immersion blender, pulse mixture for 15 seconds, or until fully blended.

4. Add 2 drops extra-virgin olive oil and blend for 10 seconds.

5. Add 2 more drops extra-virgin olive oil and blend for 10 seconds.

6. Continue adding oil 1 teaspoon at a time and blending at 10-second intervals until a mayonnaise consistency begins to form.

7. At that point, pour in remaining extra-virgin olive oil and blend until fully incorporated.

44. SHAVED BRUSSELS WITH LEMON AND PARSLEY

RICH AND ROBUST LEBANESE SEVEN-SPICE BLEND SEASONS EARTHY MUSHROOMS AND TOMATOES, WHICH ARE BAKED INSIDE VIBRANT PURPLE EGGPLANT.

SERVES 4

INGREDIENTS

2 LB. (1KG) FRESH BRUSSELS SPROUTS, TRIMMED

1 TB. EXTRA–VIRGIN OLIVE OIL

1/4 CUP FRESH PARSLEY, CHOPPED

JUICE OF 1 LEMON (ABOUT 2 TB.)

1/4 TSP. SEA SALT

1/4 TSP. FRESHLY GROUND BLACK PEPPER

1/2 CUP TOASTED HAZELNUTS, CHOPPED

DIRECTION

1. Shred Brussels sprouts using a mandoline or the grater plate of a food processor, or by slicing thinly with a knife.
2. Place a large skillet over medium heat. When the skillet is hot, add extra-virgin olive oil and wait 30 seconds.
3. Add Brussels sprouts and sauté, stirring frequently, for 1 to 2 minutes, or until sprouts are vivid green but still crisp.
4. Stir in flat-leaf parsley, lemon juice, sea salt, and black pepper. Remove from heat. Top with toasted hazelnuts to serve.

VARIATION: TO MAKE SHAVED BRUSSELS AND APPLE WITH BASIL, SUBSTITUTE FRESH BASIL FOR AT–LEAF PARSLEY, AND GRATE A FRESH APPLE TO ADD IN TO BRUSSELS SPROUTS JUST BEFORE SERVING FOR A HINT OF SWEETNESS.

THIS RECIPE PROVES THAT BRUSSELS SPROUTS DON'T HAVE TO BE FULLY COOKED TO BE ENJOYABLE. RAW BRUSSELS SPROUTS ARE AN EXCELLENT SALAD OR SLAW BASE, AND ADD A BIT OF COLOR VARIETY AND A LOT OF FRESH CRUNCH TO ANY VEGETABLE MIX.

45. Stuffed Eggplant with Lebanese Seven-Spice Blend

These sometimes spicy, sometimes mild seasonal peppers are pan roasted to perfection and tossed in nothing more than good olive oil and coarse sea salt.

SERVES 4

INGREDIENTS

2 TB. PLUS 1 TSP. EXTRA-VIRGIN OLIVE OIL

1 TSP. SEA SALT

1/2 TSP. FRESHLY GROUND BLACK PEPPER

1 MEDIUM YELLOW ONION, DICED

4 GARLIC CLOVES, MINCED

1 LB. (450G) MEDIUM CREMINI MUSHROOMS, DICED

2 MEDIUM TOMATOES, DICED

1 TB. LEBANESE SEVEN-SPICE BLEND

1/4 CUP AT-LEAF PARSLEY, CHOPPED

1/4 CUP CILANTRO, CHOPPED

2 TB. PINE NUTS, CHOPPED

DIRECTION

1. Cut eggplants in half lengthwise.
2. Using a spoon, scoop out and discard seeds and flesh, leaving a 1/2- inch (1.25cm) rim of eggplant.
3. Brush inside of each half lightly with 1 teaspoon extra-virgin olive oil. Sprinkle with 1/2 teaspoon sea salt and black pepper.
4. Place halves face up in a shallow baking dish. Bake for 15 to 20 minutes, or until lightly golden brown.
5. Meanwhile, place a medium skillet over medium-high heat. When it's hot, add 2 tablespoons extra-virgin olive oil and wait 30 seconds.
6. Add yellow onion, garlic, and mushrooms, and sauté, stirring, for 4 to 6 minutes, or until onion is translucent and mushrooms are soft.
7. Add tomatoes, Lebanese seven-spice blend, and remaining 1/2 teaspoon sea salt, and cook for 5 minutes, stirring frequently. Remove from heat. Stir in flat-leaf parsley and cilantro.
8. Remove golden eggplant halves from the oven. Reduce the oven temperature to 350°F (180°C).
9. Spoon vegetable mixture evenly into hollowed-out eggplant halves.
10. Sprinkle with pine nuts.
11. Line the baking dish with aluminum foil and place eggplant halves on top.
12. Bake for 15 to 20 minutes, or until halves are tender.
13. Let cool slightly before serving.

46. ROASTED PADRÓNS WITH SEA SALT

MAKE SURE TO KEEP THE PEPPER STEMS INTACT. THEY MAKE EXCELLENT HANDLES FOR HOLDING THE WARM PEPPERS.

SERVES 4

INGREDIENTS

1 LB. (450G) WHOLE PADRÓN PEPPERS

1 TB. HIGH-QUALITY EXTRA-VIRGIN OLIVE OIL

1⁄2 TSP. COARSE SEA SALT

DIRECTION

1. Place a medium cast-iron skillet over medium- high heat.
2. When the skillet is hot, place as many whole Padrón peppers on the bottom of the skillet as will fit. Keep a large bowl nearby, as well as a pair of tongs.
3. Cook peppers for 4 to 6 minutes, or until skins begin to blister and brown.
4. Carefully flip peppers as needed to cook all sides evenly.
5. Remove peppers to the bowl when uniformly browned and blistered.
6. Repeat with any remaining peppers.
7. When all peppers have been cooked, add high-quality extra-virgin olive oil and sea salt, and toss to combine.
8. Serve whole peppers immediately with a small bowl on the side to collect discarded stems.

47. FENNEL WITH TARRAGON AND SPICED PECANS

SERVE WARM AND TOP WITH SPICED PECANS.

SERVES 4

INGREDIENTS

4 SMALL FENNEL BULBS (OR 2 LARGE BULBS)

1 TB. EXTRA–VIRGIN OLIVE OIL

1⁄4 TSP. SEA SALT

2 TSP. FRESH TARRAGON, CHOPPED

2 TB. FRESH ORANGE JUICE

DIRECTION

1. Trim fronds and thinner stalks off each fennel bulb. Also trim each stem end.
2. Cut halves into 1⁄4-inch (.5cm) slices, removing tough inner core as you slice.
3. In a medium bowl, combine extra- virgin olive oil, sea salt, and tarragon.
4. Add fennel and toss to coat completely.
5. Place a large cast-iron skillet over medium heat. When the skillet is hot, add fennel mixture and sauté, stirring frequently, for 15 to 20 minutes, or until golden brown and caramelized.
6. Add orange juice to the hot skillet and stir, scraping any browned bits off the bottom of the skillet.

48. SPICED PECANS

2 CUPS   *20 MINUTES*
1⁄4 CUP   *5 MINUTES*

SERVES 4

INGREDIENTS

2 TB. COCONUT SUGAR

1⁄2 TSP. SEA SALT

1⁄2 TSP. CAYENNE PEPPER

1⁄4 TSP. ALLSPICE

1⁄2 TSP. CINNAMON

2 CUPS RAW PECAN HALVES

1 EGG WHITE, SLIGHTLY BEATEN

DIRECTION

1. Preheat the oven to 300°F (150°C).
2. Cut a piece of parchment paper to line the bottom of a large rimmed baking sheet (or use a silicone sheet liner).
3. In a medium bowl, combine coconut sugar, sea salt, cayenne pepper, allspice, and cinnamon.
4. In a separate bowl, toss pecans in egg white to coat completely.
5. Using a slotted spoon or fork, remove pecans and toss in seasoning mixture.
6. Spread coated pecans on the baking sheet.
7. Bake for about 20 minutes, stirring occasionally, until crisp.
8. Serve by sprinkling on Fennel with Tarragon.

49. CAULIFLOWER STEAKS WITH RAS EL HANOUT

To make Paprika Cauliflower Steaks, simply replace Ras el Hanout and cayenne pepper with 1 tablespoon smoked paprika, 1 teaspoon ground cumin, and 2 teaspoons granulated garlic.

SERVES 4

INGREDIENTS

3 TSP. EXTRA–VIRGIN OLIVE OIL

2 TB. RAS EL HANOUT

1⁄4 TSP. CAYENNE PEPPER

1⁄2 TSP. SEA SALT

DIRECTION

1. Cut cauliflower head through stem into 1¼-inch (3cm) slices. You may wish to cut it in half first, to make it easier to slice.
2. In a small bowl, combine 1 teaspoon extra-virgin olive oil, ras el hanout, cayenne pepper, and sea salt. Rub mixture on all sides of cauliflower steaks.
3. Place a large skillet over medium- high heat. When the skillet is hot, add remaining 2 teaspoons extra- virgin olive oil and wait 30 seconds.
4. Place cauliflower steaks in hot oil.
5. Fry without moving for 2 to 3 minutes, or until dark golden brown.
6. Turn steaks and cook for an additional 2 to 3 minutes on remaining side.
7. Steamed greens, or another vegetable side.

50. Spring Peas and Pearl Onions with Mint

IF YOU'D LIKE TO SKIP ANY EXTRA NITRATES THAT CAN BE NATURALLY FOUND OR ADDED IN CURED PORK PRODUCTS, FEEL FREE TO SUBSTITUTE 1⁄4 CUP SLICED AND PITTED BLACK OLIVES INSTEAD TO STILL GET THAT SALTY COMPONENT.

SERVES 4

INGREDIENTS

8 SMALL PEARL ONIONS, QUARTERED 4 CUPS FRESH SPRING PEAS, STEMS TRIMMED

V 4 TSP. SEA SALT

V 8 TSP. FRESHLY GROUND BLACK PEPPER

10 MINT LEAVES, CHOPPED 1 TSP. FRESH LEMON JUICE

V 2 OZ. (14G) SERRANO HAM OR PROSCIUTTO, fiNELY CHOPPED (OPTIONAL)

DIRECTION

1. Cut a piece of parchment paper to line the bottom of a large rimmed baking sheet (or use a silicone sheet liner).
2. In a large bowl, toss extra-virgin olive oil, pearl onions, spring peas, sea salt, and black pepper until vegetables are fully coated. Spread vegetables out evenly on the sheet.
3. Bake for 8 minutes. Remove the sheet from the oven, stir with a wooden spoon, and return to the oven for 8 to 10 minutes, or until vegetables are tender.
4. Hand lemon juice, and top with serrano ham (if using).
5. Serve warm.

CPSIA information can be obtained
at www.ICGtesting.com
Printed in the USA
BVHW021339270421
605941BV00004B/315